The
CYCLE OF
VICTORIOUS
LIVING

The CYCLE OF VICTORIOUS LIVING

Earl Lee
Hazel Lee

Beacon Hill Press of Kansas City
Kansas City, Missouri

Copyright 1971, 1995
by Beacon Hill Press of Kansas City

Revised edition 1995

ISBN 083-410-2757

Continuing Lay Training Unit 110.07A

Printed in the
United States of America

Cover design: Michael Walsh

Lee, Earl G.
    The cycle of victorious living / Earl G. Lee, Hazel Lee.—Rev. ed.

    p.   cm.
    ISBN 0-8341-0275-7
    1. Christian life—Church of the Nazarene authors. 2. Bible. O.T. Psalms XXXVII—Devotional use. 3. Peace of mind—Religious aspects—Christianity. I. Lee, Hazel. II. Title.
BV4501.2.L424   1995
248.4'8799—dc20   95-46083
                                                  CIP

10   9   8   7   6   5   4   3

Do not fret because of evildoers, nor be envious of the workers of iniquity.

For they shall soon be cut down like the grass, and wither as the green herb.

Trust in the LORD, and do good; dwell in the land, and feed on His faithfulness.

Delight yourself also in the LORD, and He shall give you the desires of your heart.

Commit your way to the LORD, trust also in Him, and He shall bring it to pass.

He shall bring forth your righteousness as the light, and your justice as the noonday.

Rest in the LORD, and wait patiently for Him; do not fret because of him who prospers in his way, because of the man who brings wicked schemes to pass.

—Ps. 37:1-7, NKJV

Contents

Foreword

The population of the world has never been greater than it is today. And yet, comparatively speaking, there have never been fewer people who believe in life—true life.

They are not confident of life because they are not committed to Life: "I am the way, the truth, and the life" (John 14:6, KJV). As one of them put it pathetically, "The only thing I wanted out of life was to get out of it." He wanted escape, not engagement. Engagement means to be *geared in, involved, going ahead.*

Earl Lee has found true life in Christ. *The Cycle of Victorious Living* presents four insights of true life from the 37th psalm. In this modest "testament of devotion," his primary interest is not to put forth a doctrine but to describe a style of life. Through his simple, straightforward words, this author's outgoing pastoral concern points the reader to the Way, the Truth, and the Life—Christ himself.

—Paul S. Rees

A Personal Note

When Beacon Hill Press of Kansas City called to say they would be reissuing *The Cycle of Victorious Living,* we were surprised. They invited us to revise portions of the book and add new material we felt would be relevant.

After much thought and prayer, we decided to leave the book largely as it was, with a few new thoughts, a new introductory chapter, and a new last chapter

It is now 1995. The book was first published in 1971 with a foreword by Paul S. Rees, now in heaven. His words remain timely.

Perhaps a whole new generation will find through a renewed edition the secret of the transcendent grace of God, which enables us to live in victorious and holy living above the turmoil and changes of these days.

(We will be writing interchangeably, without reference to which of us is sharing.)

—Earl and Hazel Lee

Preface

In 1960 I entered into a new level of life in the Spirit. I had recently completed my second term as a missionary in India and had begun deputation work in the United States. Before I left India, the Holy Spirit had confirmed to me that I would not be returning for a third term. This revelation was extremely jolting to me. First, I loved India and had found a satisfying way of life there. Second, I did not eagerly anticipate facing a new direction in midlife. As our ship left India, a fellow missionary made the sign of the cross with her hands. Little did she know how appropriate her farewell was.

"What are your plans for the future?" I was repeatedly asked during those deputation days. Although I tried to explain the unusual direction of the Spirit's guidance in my life, people's baffled looks only added to my increasing frustration. It did not make sense to them or to me, and I became desperate in my spirit.

In October 1960, while on a missionary tour in Oklahoma, I told the Lord I needed a settled spirit and a sure promise. The answer I received was so quietly simple that I hardly knew God had spoken. His word to me was "You have My will *for today*. I will take care of tomorrow."

I felt great inner relaxation as God brought my living to its least common denominator—His will for today. That was all that was necessary. Although it would be more than nine months before I was to have any idea what the future held for me and my family, that day I entered into a new level of living. It was a move upward in my spirit, much like ships moving from one lock to another in a canal. The truths that came to me through this experience are "the cycle of victorious living."

The diagram of "the cycle of victorious living" comes from the truths of Ps. 37. It illustrates the smooth sequence of living in a spiritual orbit. *Fret* always takes us out of orbit. But we can remain in the cycle by *committing, trusting, delighting,* and finally *resting.* Jesus Christ is the great Center of victorious living. The phrase "in the Lord" (or "to the Lord") is the key thought. I trust that a deeper examination of these truths in the following chapters will lead others into a new level of dynamic, Spirit-filled life in Christ.

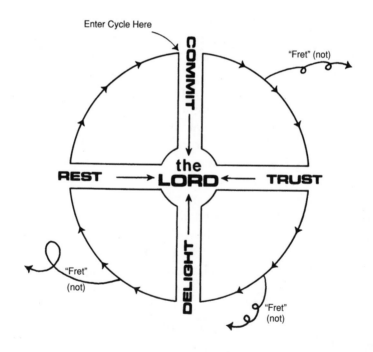

Acknowledgments

Our sincere thanks

—to Eleanor Crane and Betty Corbin for the hours they spent in typing the original as well as the revised *Cycle of Victorious Living.*

—to the late Dorothy Kejmar, who gave us permission to include her song "Live Now in Me," which was born after an exposure to the "Cycle of Victorious Living" message given at Pasadena, Calif., First Church of the Nazarene.

Note to the reader:

Live Now in Me

(Dedicated to Pastor Earl G. Lee)

D. C. K.
From Psalms 37: 3—7

Dorothy C. Kejmar

1. Com - mit thy way un - to the Lord, Com - mit thy walk
2. Trust in the Lord Thy way He planned; So shalt thou dwell
3. De - light thy - self in the dear Lord, Thy heart's de - sire

un - to His Word, And as each day you walk in Him
with - in the land. And do thou good as He has said;
firm in His Word. Rest in the Lord let fret - ting cease;

REFRAIN

Thy righ - teous light goes forth through Him. Live now in me, live now in
And ver - i - ly thou shalt be fed. (3) Com-mit and trust, de-light and
He will give blest, a - bun - dant peace.

me; With - in this seek - ing heart, Thy love di - vine im-part. Lord, teach me
rest; With - in this prais - ing heart, Thy peace di - vine im-part. Live now in

how to learn and grow, And in my walk with Thee, Thy beau-ty show.
me vic - to - rious - ly, That oth - ers now may see Thy life thro' me.

1

Rhythm—Heartbeat of God

With Jesus Christ as Lord of our lives in this cycle of victorious living, we move into a very beautiful, rhythmic pattern centering around Him and His will for us. This cycle is neither automated nor automatic. It is not motorized. It is flesh and bones and brain and heart, moved by the winds of the Spirit. It is the relation of part to part and of parts to whole. "Commit" is related to "trust," "trust" to "delight," "delight" to "rest," all parts of the Author of wholeness, Jesus Christ. Through the power of His Holy Spirit, we have symmetry, balance, and rhythm in our Christian living.

Health is a sense of rhythm in the body. Scientists call it *circadian rhythm.* The body functions as a happy, healthy unit. Sickness breaks this rhythm, causing discomfort, pain, or even death.

In my spiritual rhythm, fret can enter at any time, causing discomfort and pain. Unless the problem is detected and handled, all the spiritual balance in my life stops functioning. I must face the situation, pray and seek divine help, and again commit the matter or person to the Lord. One of my parishioners said to me quite recently, "Pastor, 'Why?' is the worst fret-trap of them all!"

The Scriptures are full of beautiful rhythmic expressions and promises. One of the most forceful is Gen. 8:22, God's promise to Noah after the Flood:

> As long as the earth endures,
> seedtime and harvest,
> cold and heat,
> summer and winter,
> day and night
> will never cease.

In the simplicity of these words lies the rhythm of sunrise and sunset, the rhythm of the tides and the moon, the revolving of the seasons, and all the magnificence of God the Creator in divine patterns in His universe.

In Acts 10:38 Peter proclaims, "God anointed Jesus of Nazareth with the Holy Spirit and power, and . . . he went around doing good . . . because God was with him."

The beauty of the rhythm of our Lord's life centering around His Father in heaven is revealed in how "he went around doing good." He is our Example, enabling us to live like Him in the power of His Spirit.

As you think about the cycle of victorious living, you can almost hear the hum of a spinning wheel:

> Commit—to the Lord
> Trust—in the Lord
> Delight—in the Lord
> Rest—in the Lord

The fabric of life, the warp and woof of living, is found in Ps. 37.

In a favorite "Peanuts" cartoon, Sally is lying in bed with that funny look on her face that only Charles Schulz can draw. She says, "My alarm didn't go off." She gets up and walks toward Charlie Brown, who is holding a bowl of cereal in his hand. She holds the alarm clock and says, "Maybe I wound it too tight . . . Sometimes if you wind an alarm clock too tight, it won't go off." As Charlie Brown eats his cereal, he mutters to himself, "We're all a little that way!"

Winding a clock too tightly can stop the rhythmic ticking or even break the mainspring. One definition for responsibility is "response-ability." The greatest response-ability I have is to hand everything over to God with no strings attached; otherwise, there is always the danger of tripping over the string.

Do you remember the fun of jumping rope? The whole game depended on the rhythmic turning of the rope and how carefully you gathered up your whole self to jump into the center without dragging a foot. It's almost as though Paul had hold of one end of the rope and the Lord had the other as he wrote, "Rejoice in the Lord always," and he keeps on turning the rope as he adds, "I will say it again: Rejoice! . . . Do not be anxious about anything, but in everything, by prayer and petition, with thanksgiving, present your requests to God. And the peace of God, which transcends all understanding, will guard your hearts and your minds in Christ Jesus" (Phil. 4:4, 6-7).

The grace of God puts rhythm into our lives. Hear it in this verse: "But if we walk in the light, as he is in the light, we have fellowship with one another, and the blood of Jesus, his Son, purifies us from all sin" (1 John 1:7). What rhythm!

A good walker paces himself into a pattern of sheer enjoyment, and everything he sees adds to his joy: flowers, mountains, birds, streams—or even cars, people, and city lawns. We have fellowship and are kindred spirits with all mankind and nature as we walk in the beautiful light of God.

I was clearing my luggage on the docks of Bombay in 1952 when, to my amazement, I saw one of the huge freight cars being moved along the tracks, not by an engine, but by 20 young workers! I could hear their low, rhythmic chant as they leaned forward, chanted, rested, leaned again, and pushed, doing the seemingly impossible in one mighty, unified effort, bound together with song.

There are rhythms that help us to "draw on our innermost." Grace works in our hearts in both joy and sorrow. When sorrow strikes us, we cry out with George Herbert: "Who would have thought my shriveled heart could have recovered greenness?" But the rhythm of life moves on, thank God, and spring comes again after a cold, barren winter.

There are many sayings ascribed to Jesus that are not written in the Gospels. One of these statements has a deep truth in it: "Turn over any stone, and I am there." No matter how hard the situation, nor how remote the territory, Jesus is always previous!

When you've been living victoriously, then a catastrophe blots your spiritual light, you feel you've lost your way. Where do you start? Where do you turn? I know no better answer than to do the next thing that has to be done. It will probably be a small and menial task, such as fixing a meal, washing a window, making a bed, driving your car to work, or facing "faceless" people. Just keep on turning over the stones as you come to them. You'll find God there—and there—and there. For He promised, "Never will I leave you" (Heb. 13:5). Continue to keep the first thrust of the cycle in operation—commit.

"Why did it happen to me?" Commit!

"There's no fair play in life!" Commit!

"I've always tried to obey God. What did I do wrong?" Commit!

"It doesn't pay to take up your cross. Everything is topsy-turvy." Commit!

"Help me, Lord. I've lost my way. I'm out of touch with You and Your will." Commit. Trust. Delight in the Lord. "Thank You, Jesus. By faith I know You are there." Commit. Trust. Delight. Rest. Rest? Yes, rest in the Lord. The old freight train will begin to move down the tracks. The jump rope will begin to turn. The spinning wheel will start to hum.

The most difficult experience in life to find our way through is sorrow. A deep undercurrent of sorrow is a part of living for all of us sooner or later. The dictionary defines sorrow as "the deep, often long-continued mental anguish caused by a sense of loss, disappointment, remorse, or regret." There is a strange rhythm in sorrow. Tides of suffering move in and out of our lives. At sorrow's full tide, it's good to know where the answer lies. We can know that in the darkness the Lord is standing by, regardless of whether or not we can see Him. And one day, even as tides recede, so the rhythm of release begins as we place the entire sorrow into the nail-pierced hands of the One who understands. "Surely he took up our infirmities and carried our sorrows" (Isa. 53:4).

In the time of sorrow, how can we delight in the Lord? Heb. 13:15 tells us: "Through Jesus, therefore, let us continually offer to God a sacrifice of praise." It is a divine privilege to share in the sufferings of Christ, thus making our sorrow redemptive. Our delight comes from the awareness that we are being conformed into His image.

If sorrow becomes redemptive, we in turn are able to "comfort those in any trouble with the comfort we ourselves have received from God" (2 Cor. 1:4). Our Lord knew the underside of suffering. One day on a hillside He looked upon the multitudes with compassion as He said, "Blessed are those who mourn, for they will be comforted" (Matt 5:4). Is there any comfort quite so healing as to be able, once again, to reach out and touch our brother's or sister's need?

A young man stricken with a fatal illness was writing to a friend about the short time he had left to live. In his letter he expressed his firm faith with these words: "God's love is deeper than the deepest sea, and it has no ebb or flow." What confidence!

In order to have true rhythm, there must be a constant, an absolute. Such is the great love of God. He is always there, and in Him there is "no variableness, neither shadow of turning" (James 1:17, KJV).

The cycle of victorious living revolves around the love of God. That's where the rhythm begins—out of the heartbeat of God—and that's where it returns.

2

Do Not Fret

Years ago I was asked by a religious organization to speak on the subject of victorious living. Through a printer's error, the subject was announced as "The Cycle of *Victorian* Living." I was quite amused as I read the card. The Christian life is *not* Victorian living—a life of continual negatives, prohibitions, inhibitions, and long-faced properness. People who, as Thoreau phrased it, "lead lives of quiet desperation" are a part of the problem of religious life today. They fret. God wants us to be free from continual fretting. He has made provision for abundant living through the power of the Holy Spirit in the fully yielded heart.

Can we live completely free of fret? First, we must understand the meaning of "fret." One person's "fret" is another person's "legitimate concern." Regardless of how we interpret the word, one vital truth is clear: The Holy Spirit does not want our spiritual life to become frayed. "Do not fret" is more than a pastoral directive; it is a divine imperative.

David faced a legitimate concern in Ps. 37. You would think he had access to one of our daily newspapers as he wrote about the ungodly prospering and evil people standing in the way of the righteous. Yet his opening admonition is "Do not fret."

In writing to the Philippians, Paul said, "Do not be anxious about anything" (4:6), or, as *The Living Bible* translates

it, "Don't worry about anything; instead, pray about everything; tell God your needs and don't forget to thank him for
his answers. If you do this you will experience God's peace,
which is far more wonderful than the human mind can understand. His peace will keep your thoughts and your
hearts quiet and at rest as you trust in Christ Jesus" (vv. 6-
7). Over and over again we are pointed to the great Center,
Christ Jesus.

Paul did not write these words from a plush hotel—he
was in jail. But the tone and message of the entire letter to
the Philippians shows that Paul had found his cycle of victorious living while living in a dungeon. He used such phrases
as "Do not be anxious about anything" (4:6), "I rejoice
greatly in the Lord" (v. 10), "I can do everything through
him who gives me strength" (v. 13), "Rejoice in the Lord always" (v. 4), "The peace of God . . . will guard your hearts
and your minds" (v. 7), "My God will meet all your needs"
(v. 19), "I have learned the secret of being content in any
and every situation" (v. 12), and "To our God and Father be
glory for ever and ever" (v. 20).

The teachings of Jesus have the same familiar ring:
"Seek first his kingdom" (Matt. 6:33), "Do not worry about
tomorrow" (v. 34), "Store up for yourselves treasures in
heaven" (v. 20), "See how the lilies of the field grow" (v.
28), and "Ask and it will be given to you; seek and you will
find; knock and the door will be opened to you" (7:7).

Oswald Chambers says, "All our fret and worry is
caused by calculating without God." It destroys victorious
living as surely as insects and other pests destroy leaves.

I enjoy caring for my roses, camellias, and azaleas. One
camellia bush off in a corner of the flower bed began to
look very anemic. Weeds had sprung up around it, and it
produced only a few weak blooms. I determined to restore
its beauty. As I cleaned out the weeds, I discovered the true
cause for concern. Embedded in the soil near the roots and
on up under the leaves were a number of snails. They had
fed themselves heartily on the branches and leaves. With

the use of specially prepared pellets, the snails were soon eliminated. The blooms again became rich and colorful.

Fret is the snail under the leaf. In order to have lives of fragrance and beauty, these snails of fret must go. And God has a specially prepared way for their exit. It is found in the cycle of victorious living.

Tension is normal and natural in life. Without tension we could not exist, any more than a violin string can be played without being stretched across the bridge. Creative tension is not the same as destructive worry. Worry is like racing an automobile engine while it is in neutral. The gas, noise, and smog do not get us anywhere. But legitimate concern—creative tension—is putting the car into low gear on your way to moving ahead. Use the power God has given you to do something about the situation that could cause you to fret.

You really move into high gear when you affirm, "Now to him who is able to do immeasurably more than all we ask or imagine, according to his power that is at work within us, to him be glory" (Eph. 3:20-21). That scripture goes places, and you go with it. It's a long way from worrying, fretting, and stewing in a state of paralysis. When I know there is something that needs to be done or someone I need to see, I am miserable until I take care of the matter. Fret is often removed not by praying but by *doing*. You have to take the gearshift out of neutral, put it into low, and get going.

E. Stanley Jones tells about a bird in India that he calls a "champion pessimist." This bird goes around all day crying shrilly, "Pity-to-do-it, pity-to-do-it." At night, they say, he sleeps on his back with his long legs in the air to keep the sky from falling!

Too often we excuse ourselves by saying, "Well, I'm just a natural worrywart!" Worry should not be lightly excused. It is a malignant cancer that, left untreated, will eat down into the spirit until it destroys life. The only way to handle this critical malignancy is to let the Holy Spirit operate on it—because *fret takes us out of orbit.* It is the cell malfunctioning, refusing to work with the normal, happily functioning body cells. It has become self-centered, and its refusal to cooperate can bring death. It must be treated speedily and faced with a ruthless honesty. We are helpless to handle it alone. Only the Holy Spirit can rid the yielded spirit of fret through grace.

Fret is defined as the following: "To eat away, to gnaw, to gall, to vex, to worry, to agitate, to wear away." Jesus tells us in Mark 4:19 (Moffatt), "But the worries of the world . . . come in to choke the word." Fret includes

> **F**ear
> **R**esentment
> **E**nvy
> **T**ension (destructive)

Charlie Brown is sometimes quite a theologian. In one cartoon Linus drags his blanket as he observes, "You look kinda depressed, Charlie Brown." Charlie Brown replies, "I worry about school a lot." Then he adds, "I worry about my worrying so much about school." As they sit on a log together, Charlie Brown makes his final observation: "My anxieties have anxieties!" I shared this cartoon in one of my Sunday sermons. Soon afterward I received the following letter:

Dear Pastor Lee,
   I want to say "Praise the Lord" while it is fresh in my heart. I have been troubled by a verse for some time now. *The New English Bible* in Phil. 4:5-6 says, "The Lord is near; have no anxiety, but in everything make your requests known to God in prayer and petition with thanksgiving." God knows that I have been torn by anxiety over insignificant things. Your quote from Snoopy [Charlie Brown] about worrying about worry seemed to fit me. Your message on "Do Not Fret" was for me. I placed all my worrying and fretting on the altar and left it there, glory be to God! I now claim the above verse, for I have

come to realize that it is the second part, "with thanks-giving" and praise, that makes the first part reality.

This letter warmed my heart to see a Christian find a new level of victorious living. How wonderful to realize that "all God's commandments are His enablings"! Our Heavenly Father never asks us to do what He does not help us through His grace to do. It is a loving, providing Father who says, "Do not fret." He wants us to move into more abundant living above the smog-filled atmosphere of fret.

"Do not fret" is not an impossible way of life. There is a cycle whereby life can be continually victorious. When we realize we are becoming victims of fret, that we are getting out of orbit, we must ask forgiveness and get back into the cycle by once more committing our way to the Lord.

3

Commit—Hands Down

David says, "Commit your way to the LORD; trust in him and he will do this: He will make your righteousness shine like the dawn, the justice of your cause like the noonday sun" (Ps. 37:5-6). It all starts with commitment.

Commitment is more than a sentimental decision that may change one's life for a few emotion-filled days. It is a valid act of the will, changing one's whole way of life. It is the entrance into the cycle of victorious living.

The true meaning of the word "commit" came to me as I was reading Ps. 37 in Marathi, our "stepmother" language of India. In a free translation of the Marathi, it says, "Turn what you are and what you have over to God—palms down!" Suppose I hold a piece of chalk in my hand and ask you to take it. You reach out and take it from my upturned hand. True commitment requires me to turn my palm over and completely drop into your hand what I hold. None of it remains in my hand. This process involves an exercise of the will. It reminds me of Oswald Chambers's words: "I have nothing to do with what will happen if I obey. I must abandon myself to God's call in unconditional surrender and smilingly wash my hands of the consequences." This prayer goes beyond "You take it" to "I release it." There's quite a difference. It was this prayer that day in Oklahoma that took me into a new level of Spirit-filled living.

Commitment is both initial and continuous. We enter the cycle by commitment. The need, the problem, the urgent prayer request are all given over to God. But our minds remain quite active, and here is where Satan comes in to accuse. Whenever the temptation to fret confronts us, we must tell our adversary that the bothersome matter is now in God's hands, and that he is wasting his time in needling us.

Satan is not omniscient—he has to be told that we mean business. "Resist the devil, and he will flee from you" (James 4:7). Send him to your great Advocate, Jesus Christ. Jesus knows the set of your heart and the direction of your will. He also knows how to protect you and how to help you handle your emotions.

The will has often been compared to the rudder of a boat. But have you thought of how much more boat there is than rudder? Our emotions make up most of our conscious being. However, as Fénelon says, our will to obey God is where true religion resides.

If my reputation were being attacked by a slanderous accuser, I would not waste time talking to him. I would place my case into the hands of a competent attorney and refer my adversary to him. When you are tempted to relive all the pre-commitment days, the pain and the struggle, and feel the slight edge of doubt moving in, remember that you have an Advocate, and call on Him—"Thank You, Lord—I believe!"

Osterly's translation of the Hebrew for "commit" has important significance for Christians. "It takes on the idea of to roll, whirl, turn . . . the wholehearted flinging of oneself upon God, knowing that His will prevails."

As J. Edwin Orr was struggling to be filled with the Spirit, he prayed, "Now, Lord, I will give You my business." But nothing happened. In the throes of making a decision concerning a life's companion, he added, "Lord, I will give her to You." Still nothing happened. One day, in desperation, he cried, "Lord, I give You my choice of a career." Still nothing happened. Finally, he completely let go and prayed, "Lord, I give You myself. I commit to You my will, and You have *me*." With this total commitment, the Holy Spirit came in cleansing power.

While visiting the space center at Cape Canaveral, Fla., we were impressed by the ingenuity of humans as they have sought to discover secrets of our universe. We read the checklist of items to be covered before shuttles are launched. Just before the last item on the list, "liftoff," was the one word "commit." The astronauts must mentally prepare for their launch, probably a mixture of excitement and a tinge of apprehension as a new world in outer space opens before them.

For us who follow our Lord into the adventure of victorious living, there must be a full commitment to His way and His laws. Once launched, there is a "point of no return" for the astronaut. So it is true for us who follow Christ. Commitment means looking forward as well as "forgetting those things which are behind" (Phil. 3:13, KJV).

Commitment demands responsibility and discipline. It demands a priority to the claims of Christ over our own limited desires and plans. It means to "let go and let God."

Barbara Johnson, author of *Where Does a Mother Go to Resign?* and many other books for hurting people, describes letting go:

1. To let go doesn't mean to STOP CARING; it means I can't DO IT for someone else.

2. To let go is not to CUT MYSELF OFF; it is the realization that I can't CONTROL another.

3. To let go is not to ENABLE, but to allow learning from natural CONSEQUENCES.

4. To let go is to admit POWERLESSNESS, which means the OUTCOME is not in MY hands.

5. To let go is not to try to change or BLAME another; I can ONLY change myself.

6. To let go is not to CARE FOR, but to care ABOUT.

7. To let go is not to FIX, but to be SUPPORTIVE.

8. To let go is not to JUDGE, but to allow another to be a human being.

9. To let go is not to be in the MIDDLE arranging all the outcomes, but to ALLOW others to EFFECT their own outcomes.

10. To let go is not to be PROTECTIVE; it is to permit another to face reality.

11. To let go is not to DENY, but to ACCEPT.

12. To let go is not to NAG, scold, or argue, but to SEARCH OUT MY OWN shortcomings and correct them.

13. To let go is not to ADJUST everything to my desires, but to TAKE EACH DAY as it comes, and cherish the moment.

14. To let go is not to CRITICIZE and REGULATE anyone, but to become the BEST I CAN BE.

15. To let go is not to REGRET the past, but to GROW and LIVE for the future.

16. To let go is to FEAR LESS, trust in Christ more, and freely give the love He's given to me.

True commitment means we give to Him our all—totally, not on condition. When conditions are attached, our palms are held upward. Deep commitment means our *palms are down*. It is the only way to enter the cycle of victorious living.

Oswald Chambers reminds us that we command what we understand. But commitment demands faith in the character of our God and not in the circumstances we see or understand.

Commitment is not only initial; it is continuous. We are changing, living human beings. We face new situations constantly, and over and over new problems are fed into the cycle. But the process, once learned, becomes a victorious way of life. New light comes, and specific areas are dealt with. Practical, sanctified living never "arrives" or ceases to learn and apply principles of victory.

Robert Atwood wrote an article in the *Daily Times* of Anchorage, Alaska, describing the terrible earthquake that occurred on Good Friday in 1964. He arrived home from work about 5:30 as his wife was leaving for the grocery store. He hesitated a moment as he considered going with her but decided to remain home to practice his trumpet.

I began practicing my trumpet when the earthquake started. Minor earthquakes are not uncommon here, but they've always taught me to stop what I'm doing and watch what happens. It was quickly obvious that this was no minor earthquake. The chandelier, made from a ship's wheel, swayed too much. Things were falling that had never fallen before. I headed for the door carrying my trumpet. At the door I saw a wall weaving. On the driveway I turned and watched my house swerve and groan as though in mortal agony. It was as though someone had engaged it in a gigantic taffy pull—stretching it, shrinking and twisting it. I became aware of tall trees falling in our yard, so I moved to a spot that I thought would be safe. As I moved I saw cracks appear in the earth. Pieces of ground in jigsaw shapes moved up and down, tilted at all angles.

As I started to climb the fence to my neighbor's yard, the fence disappeared. Trees were falling in crazy patterns. Deep chasms cushioned the impact. I was on the verge of a quick burial. I could not pull my right arm from the sand. It was buried to the shoulder. Most of the rest of my body was also covered. *I had to let go of my trumpet,* and my arm pulled free easily!

Often our "trumpets" are the expression of our rights, our egos, and our desire for recognition and reward. When we commit ourselves, we learn to live without "trumpets." "Take my yoke upon you and learn from me, for I am gentle and humble in heart, and you will find rest for your souls" (Matt. 11:29). It may take an earthquake upheaval to pry us loose from our "trumpets," but it is the only way that will lead to rest of soul.

As a pastor I prayed at the altar one morning with a woman seeking God's help. After a few moments she confessed that her mother was hindering her in her newly discovered Christian life. I asked if she had heard my sermon on "The Cycle of Victorious Living." She answered a faint "Yes."

"Do you believe it?" I asked.

"Yes, Pastor, I do," was her reply.

"Then, Betty, I believe what you have to do is to commit your mother as she is now to the Lord. Place her in His hands without any condition. Then leave her there. Will you do this?"

I saw a light break over her drawn face as she answered, "I will do just that—now!"

After her prayer I reminded her that the Lord was in charge of her mother and that she herself should begin to delight in the Lord and rest.

She began to thank the Lord. As she stood from the altar, she stepped into the cycle.

A week later she said, "Believe me—delighting in the Lord was the way for me and my sister to live with my mother." It works! And it begins with commitment.

The call to commitment is not from any man. It is God's call to us. His call is always total. He does not deal in partial victories nor with halfhearted surrenders. "Trumpets" have to go. Palms have to be turned down and fully opened.

Elizabeth Burns (née Gert Behanna) writes about her son Allen in *The Late Liz*. He had rejected her long before she became a Christian and had also refused all her attempts for reconciliation after her conversion. He had caused her much heartache, and she had cried over him many nights. She writes:

> Like it or not, the day came when you bent over, swept up the pieces, glued them together, and took it from there. You yourself were a matter of what you did with the pieces.
>
> If this was true of me, it was true of my sons as well. If it tore the heart out, the weight of Allen had to be lifted. The sorrow of him and of the harm I'd done him were blocks on the road to usefulness. Lift him up and let him go, *let him go*. Even if he was still alive, I still had to let him go. Allen's outcome was Allen's business. Grief could no longer block me from forgiving myself in order that I might learn to forgive all. "So, son, you are released! My love pries you loose. My love hands you over to Him Who is the Source of comfort."

Where love is involved, where loved ones tear at the heart, the prayer of commitment often includes the prayer of relinquishment. It must have been that type of prayer that Abraham prayed as he climbed the mountain with Isaac, his son and promised heir. It is one of the most difficult prayers we pray: *Lord, here it is. Lord, here he or she is. Lord, here I am. You have me.* It is the only way into the cycle.

The cycle is well summed up in the words of Jesus in John 15:4—"Remain in me, and I will remain in you. No branch can bear fruit by itself; it must remain in the vine. Neither can you bear fruit unless you remain in me." It is a cycle of abiding.

4

Trust—Lean Hard

P astor, I've really committed everything, including myself, to the Lord. Now what do I do?"

"There is only one thing to do: lean hard! You have changed from independence to dependence. You don't just lean; you lean on Someone well able to carry your weight, on the One who created the heavens and the earth and who never fails."

The smile of understanding made me realize another believer had entered into the cycle.

Trust is a key word in the Psalms. It weaves in and out of the cycle. "Trust in the LORD and do good; dwell in the land and enjoy safe pasture" (Ps. 37:3).

The Amplified Bible translates trust as "lean on, rely on and be confident" (ibid.). David Livingstone literally staked his life on the words "And, lo, I am with you alway, even unto the end of the world" (Matt. 28:20, KJV). On the evening of January 14, 1856, he wrote in his diary, "It is the word of a gentleman of the most strict and sacred honour, so there's an end of it!" This immensely lonely man, dying on his knees, left a last entry in his journal in 1873: "He will keep His word, the Gracious One, full of grace and truth; no doubt about it. He will keep His word, and it will be all right. Doubt is here inadmissible, surely!" God kept His sacred pledge.

If faith is nothing apart from its object, the same is true of trust, for they are closely akin in meaning. The recommendation from Scripture is to lean hard on the Lord. He made heaven and earth. He calms the storms and stills the waves. His is the earth "and everything in it, the world, and all who live in it" (Ps. 24:1). He is the One on whom you lean—all your weight on all of Him! You feel lighter after casting your cares on the Lord. Once you find release through commitment and trust, leaning hard becomes another forward move in the cycle. Here is meaningful, sanctified living filled with adventure.

Commerce Bank and Trust Company once advertised the services of their trust department. Their ad closed with these words: "Trust us. After all, *Trust* is a very important part of our name." Would God not say to us, "Trust is a very important part of My name"?

In our fractured world it is easy to be cynical and to find very few areas in which to trust. But when we pray a prayer of commitment, we need an object for trust.

When you wait for an answer to prayer, try drawing the "triangle of trust" diagram. Draw a triangle. In the left lower angle, A, write your name. At the apex of the triangle, B, write God's name. At the right lower angle, C, write the request, the person, or the situation.

Our tendency as we pray is to keep looking at angle C— the need—and to watch for an answer. God has taught us instead to keep our eyes on the apex, angle B, and then thank Him continually for all He is doing that we know nothing about. This is an exercise of faith and hope—but it also brings great peace of mind. Praise is the key.

Trust also calls for an active response. We do not place our trust in God, sit back, and do nothing. A very important part of this transaction is expressed in the words of Mary: "Do whatever he tells you" (John 2:5). Before the water could be turned into wine, waterpots had to be filled. The Bible says for us to "trust . . . and do good" (Ps. 37:3). Doing good, having an obedient spirit, is an absolute necessity. We are freed from our burden, not to sit down, but to "run with patience the race that is set before us" (Heb. 12:1, KJV). One cannot run entangled in cumbersome cares.

Fret is a constant possibility. Satan will not cease his efforts to get us out of orbit. He usually attacks the mind with insidious little doubts that if entertained will become fret. God's command not to fret is not only a requirement for entering the cycle but also a requirement for remaining in it. The opportunity to fret will always present itself, but as trust becomes more and more our way of life, we become less aware of the assaults on our faith.

I remember very vividly how easily I could have slipped out of the cycle of victorious living as I faced a staggering problem in one of my pastorates. First a sense of concern—good, legitimate concern—settled over my spirit. It was not long before I sensed that this concern was becoming seeded with fear. The clouds lowered over me, and I moved into a gray world. In my praying I was telling the Lord everything He already knew. I was actually making my apprehension verbal and sinking into fret.

After two days of such suffering, God seemed to say to me, "Who asked you to come to this church in the first place?"

"Why, You did, Lord," I replied.

"Well, then, all you need to do is to obey Me one step at a time. Give Me the problem, and do as I say. This church does not belong to you—it belongs to Me."

I rolled each care over onto Him. Thanking Him for His faithful reminder to me that I was getting out of orbit, I found thanksgiving filling my heart.

It was the same process I followed back in 1960 while on that deputation tour. But it was a new situation, so the continuous process went on. God gloriously cared for the problem beyond all I could ask or think. Moffatt translates Ps. 37:5, "Leave all to him, rely on him, and he will see to it." And that is exactly what He did.

As a resident missionary, I was responsible for the supervision of the construction of a chapel in Basim, India, in 1950. One very hot day I stood at a distance, watching the master mason do his work. Each stone was carefully fit into place, and many hands were required to complete the job. About a dozen workers shuffled past me, carrying headloads of crushed rock, which were handed up a shaky scaffold to the mason, who properly mixed the cement and worked it around the larger, specially dressed stones. I did not realize the importance of the workers until the Lord and I had a conversation.

"How closely you watch the master mason!" He said.

"Yes, Lord. He's an artist, and his work is fascinating."

"But you've paid no attention to the workers shuffling along beside you, have you?"

I was taken aback a bit as I said, "Workers? Yes, but what they're doing doesn't interest me like the skilled work of the mason."

Then He got all my attention as the lesson He was teaching me came through: "Son, you are nothing but a servant in My kingdom. I am the Master Mason. Keep on handing Me what I need, and I will see that the Kingdom is built."

How many times since that hot day have I reminded myself that I am nothing but a servant! And again the deep meaning of the phrase in verse 5 burned into my spirit: "Trust . . . and he will do this."

Paul expressed the same thought in a familiar scripture: "I planted, Apollos watered, but God [all the while] was making it grow, and [He] gave the increase" (1 Cor. 3:6, Amp.).

5

Delight—Look Up

Delight is far more than an emotion. It is an attitude of the spirit. The Psalmist said, "I delight to do thy will, O my God" (40:8, KJV). God's will is many times not what we would choose. Yet David says in Ps. 37:4 for us to delight ourselves *in the Lord,* not in circumstances, successes, or honors. We must often bring our emotions into line by our will.

A store in the process of being remodeled posted this sign: "Under New Attitude." That sign opened up a whole new thought regarding some drastic change going on. It was a refreshing insight.

In 1962 John Glenn was given the historic and dangerous mission of circling our world. A friend and I listened anxiously to my radio. The man in control from the space center in Houston commanded Glenn, "Change your attitude two degrees toward Houston." I was surprised that in such a historic and critical event he had mistakenly said "attitude" when it would appear he meant "altitude." But my more knowledgeable friend said, "Oh, that's exactly what he meant."

"Change your attitude toward Houston." Houston was the center of the operation, right where everything had been planned, practiced, and rehearsed for many months. Quickly, with no discussion, John Glenn replied, "Yes, sir—attitude changed two degrees toward Houston." And in a short period of time, "Mission accomplished" were the simple but great words heard around the world.

How many times have I heard the whisper of the Holy Spirit, "Change your attitude so many degrees toward God"? God's love is the measuring instrument, and He demands that we line up perfectly. We will never hear "Mission accomplished" until He is finished with us on the earth. Until then, we must continue adjusting our attitude. The attitude of the cycle of victorious living is delight.

The clouds hung low one year in India. Hazel and our infant son were ill, and it seemed impossible to penetrate heaven with our prayers. We were pressed beyond measure. One hot, still morning she came to me with the baby in her arms and said, "Take care of him for a while; I must find my way through this darkness. I'm going to pray and not return until I've found an answer."

Her experience is best expressed in these words she wrote afterward:

> I closed the door and knelt down by the bed and cried out my heart's agony. "O God, show me the way through, for I have no way to turn!" As I waited, a quiet voice spoke to me, "Look on the table beside the bed. You'll see the answer there."
>
> I was a bit startled but stood and walked over to the little night table. A small book lay on the table, and the title, in letters of fire, read *REJOICE*. Then God spoke to me again, saying, "Here is the way through; praise Me and delight in Me for myself alone, and I will come to your rescue."
>
> It sounds easy when one writes it, but to practice praise under the circumstances took a bit of rethinking. I had been so consumed by the pressures of the problem as well as extreme physical weakness that to be able to express joy seemed an impossibility.
>
> As I knelt again to pray, I was reminded by the Lord of my grandmother. My grandparents gave more than 20 years of their lives as missionaries in the north part of India.

During the latter years of her life, my grandmother came to live with my mother. I loved her dearly and enjoyed talking to her about her many experiences as a missionary. She was afflicted with severe attacks of asthma. Many times I heard the sound of her thin little voice in the early morning gasping out between painful wheezings, "Praise the Lord! Hallelujah! Glory to God!"

One morning, as I took her breakfast tray to her, I was deeply upset, and I asked rather exasperatedly, "Grandma, what do you have to praise the Lord for? Why are you using your strength like this?" To my young mind, things did not add up.

She smiled as she looked at me and said, "I praise God for who He is, not for what comes into my life! I guess you would call it the sacrifice of praise. It brings peace to my heart and makes the suffering easier to bear."

Now many years later, far away in a foreign land, the memory returned to me and the great lesson it taught. The sacrifice of praise—how wonderful!

After asking forgiveness, I began to praise the Lord with a heart filled with gratitude for *all He was to me.* Soon the brassy heavens began to melt, and a shower of glory fell around my soul, and the clouds of depression and darkness vanished into the sunlight of His presence.

As my wife shared this experience with me, we both turned a corner into a new way of life. It was the way of *purposeful delight.*

The Psalmist also reminds us that if we delight in the Lord, we will have the desires of our hearts. God also purifies those desires so that what we want comes into line with His perfect will.

Phil. 4:4 says, "Rejoice in the Lord always. I will say it again: Rejoice!" Satan continually tries to blur this great truth of delighting in the Lord. Too often we forget to rejoice in the Lord. We must remember to say, "Thank You" with our praise. We must revere the Giver more than His gift.

Delighting in the Lord means:

> **D**aily
> **E**verything
> **L**aid
> **I**nto
> **G**od's
> **H**ands
> **T**riumphantly

The matter of delighting daily and *triumphantly* keeps us in the cycle of victorious living with increased momentum.

When we delight in the Lord, we lift up our eyes with deliberate intent. It is a matter of the will, not the emotions. But it often refreshingly affects the emotions.

Paul tells us to "be transformed by the renewing of your mind" (Rom. 12:2). Delighting in the Lord is a process; it is a practice and can become a splendid habit. "The Song of the Lark" is a painting depicting a young gleaner standing in the field with upturned face, her monotonous work forgotten for a brief moment as she listens to the musical call of a lark. Delighting in the Lord is hearing His call in the middle of life's humdrum and responding with an upturned spirit of praise.

The dimension of delight is actually limitless. Like circling ripples in a lake, it reaches to the very shores of heaven. There is a running-over, effervescent quality about it that spills over into a divine certainty. J. B. Phillips translates Rom. 8:38-39, "I have become absolutely convinced that neither death nor life, neither messenger of Heaven nor monarch of earth, neither what happens today nor what may happen tomorrow, neither a power from on high nor a power from below, nor anything else in God's whole world has any power to separate us from the love of God in Christ Jesus our Lord!"

What a joyous declaration of faith! *Faith*—not circumstances—makes joy possible. The Center of our joy is Jesus Christ, the Son of God.

A detour along a highway implies that the regular, direct route is closed. Our enemy seeks to place detour signs on the highway of holy living that say, "Take this roundabout way. Deviate from the direct path." Detours from delight plunge us into the bumpy road of fret, and there is nothing to do but to back up, confess our need, and continue on the high road, blessing the Lord at all times with His Word continually in our mouths (see Ps. 34:1, KJV).

In 2 Chron. 20, singers were appointed who were to praise the Lord in "the beauty of holiness" (v. 21, KJV). Verse 22 says, "As they began to sing and praise, the LORD set ambushes against the men of Ammon . . . and they were defeated." Jehoshaphat would never have known victory from the enemy without these songs of praise. It is also *our* best way to overcome our enemy. Delight is demonstrated in victory. After we stop fretting, commit our way to the Lord, and trust in Him, we are able to rejoice in Him who is "the delight of our life as well as the life of our delight."

Delight is contagious. We can be carriers of the delight of the Lord. When I was a boy, our home was stricken with diphtheria, and it was discovered that I was the carrier of this disease. Our world needs Christians filled with delight, exposing people to it wherever they go—in schools and hospitals, at desks, in garages and shops—people contagious for Christ. God wants us to be delightful Christians—delight-filled.

Unfortunately, we cannot get an injection of delight. The villagers we encountered during our years in India never felt they had been properly treated by their doctor unless they received an injection. They could be given a handful of pills with explicit directions, but unless they got an injection, they were not satisfied. God's way is a handful of directives, and unless we follow Him explicitly, there can be no delight. It is through obedience that we discover joy. C. S. Lewis defined praise as "inner health made audible." It is not an isolated experience—it is a way of life.

It is best, as F. B. Meyer expressed it, to "keep short accounts with God." It is good to have a daily check during our devotions to see if we are delighting in the Lord. There must be no hidden, unclean corners, no sweeping of life under the

rug. **D**aily **E**verything **L**aid **I**nto **G**od's **H**ands **T**riumphantly—
our finances, our mental life, our homelife, our business, our
friends, and our associates. Nothing can be left out.

One translator uses for "delight" the word "relish." It im-
plies something of a distinct flavor that we enjoy tasting.
David said, "Taste and see that the LORD is good" (Ps. 34:8).
His taste is not bitter and sour, but flavorful and sweet.

What must our Master think when He looks into our shriveled hearts so lacking in praise and joyousness? It seems that
we know everything about life in the Spirit except how to live
it! With gracious understanding He will teach us how to live
victoriously, that we might "bear much fruit" (John 15:5, 8).

John Philip Sousa, known as the March King, was surprised one day to hear floating up into his hotel room the
strains of his favorite march, "Stars and Stripes Forever." It
was being played at a slow, lazy, dragging tempo by an organ-
grinder in the street below. He dashed down into the street.
"Here, here!" he called to the sleepy organ-grinder. "That's no
way to play my march!" He seized the handle and turned it
vigorously. The music came out spirited and happy, and the
little organ-grinder smiled and bowed low to Mr. Sousa.

The next night Mr. Sousa heard his song again, but this
time the tempo was right. He looked out his window and no-
ticed a large sign with the organ-grinder's name and under-
neath the words "pupil of John Philip Sousa."

When we delight in the Lord—and we must—we will
write under the joys of our lives, "pupil of Jesus Christ."

What about receiving the desires of our hearts? Strangely
enough, before we learn this secret of delight, we are inclined
to concentrate primarily on all the things we would like to
have. But after delight becomes a way of life, after we learn
the secret of victorious living in the Spirit, our lives become
unidirectional—we want most of all to be like Him and to live
out His love for others. Everything else becomes a happy
extra.

6

Rest—Cash In

While my family and I were vacationing in beautiful British Columbia, we visited a special farm where Scottie dogs were trained to do all kinds of tricks. They were dressed up in children's clothes, made to jump through hoops, roll barrels, climb ladders, and do numerous things that dogs do not ordinarily do. The trainer always had a pocket filled with treats, and for every trick well done, the dogs were rewarded with a word of encouragement and a treat. It was the old system of reward for disciplined performance. But the reward was never given until *after* the learning attempt was made.

The Christian may well ask, "Why can't I go from commitment to rest? Why are there no immediate rewards? Why must I go through the full cycle of trust and delight?"

If we do not come by the route of trust and delight, we are hardly ready for the benefit of rest. Rest is usually hard-earned. The writer to the Hebrews admonishes, "Let us, therefore, make every effort to enter that rest" (4:11)—or, as *The Amplified Bible* says, "Let us therefore be zealous and exert ourselves and strive diligently to enter into that rest [of God]." As the man who has come up the hard way in the financial world truly appreciates the value of money, so through obedience to personal disciplines do we know the real meaning of the word "rest." There are divine patterns that must be followed, or we cannot know the joy of "cashing in" on our investment in the Spirit.

This way of life is God's will for every child of His; it is not an option. He has designed a way for us—clear, direct, and attractive. It is to our advantage to follow instructions.

Søren Kierkegaard tells the story of a wild duck who decided to alter his pattern of life. As he was flying south with his fellow ducks, he happened to see on the ground below him some corn a farmer had scattered for his barnyard fowls. So the lazy fellow fluttered down, joined the other ducks, ate the corn, and lingered on. Enjoying the food and security of the barnyard, he forgot about his flying companions and spent the winter in ease.

One spring day he heard the call of the wild ducks overhead as they were flying north. Something deep within him responded to the wild call, and he tried to spread his wings. He fluttered up the best he could, but he had grown fat and flabby and could fly only as far as the eaves of the barn. He watched with despair as his former friends disappeared into the sky, leaving him earthbound to security.

This story is too often a depiction of our lives. We are made for personal victory in Christ Jesus. The plan is clear; the cycle is obvious. Yet we have allowed some deviation to destroy the call of the sky and have succumbed to living in "barnyard security" with wings helpless because of lack of use. This condition is not resting in the Lord—it is a condition of rusting in ourselves.

The Ps. 37 rest is an *active* rest. God speaks; I listen and obey. And with each new situation, I find my way through the cycle to inner rest. It is a rest from friction, not a rest from action. Major Shupp of the United States Marine Corps said, "If we can read it, we can do it." There is a rest in doing when it is in the Lord.

Amos cries out, "Woe to them that are at ease in Zion . . . !" (6:1, KJV). This is a picture of *ease,* not of rest. There is a great difference between comforts and comfort. People can live in ease without experiencing rest. John D. Rockefeller was asked how much money it took to make a man happy. Speaking from experience, he said, "Just a little bit more!" The rest God has for us enables us to abound in fruitful and tireless service to Him.

In Ps. 37, David reminds us to "be still before the LORD and wait patiently for him" (v. 7). The root from the Hebrew for "rest" (KJV) is "to cease, to be silent, or submit in silence to what He ordains." God has directives for us that cannot be received clearly until the inner station of the heart is quiet. God's quiet voice may have something to say to us that will change our life's direction. We are never too old for this to be a possibility; it keeps a stretch of anticipation in the soul.

In recent months my mother, Estelle Crutcher, now 98, and my husband and I faced the reality that she could no longer live without nursing care. This decision is usually quite traumatic. But her realization and her complete submission to the change in her lifestyle made the process less frightening. Even so, for me there were many tears. One day after we had left her in limited space in a room with an unknown roommate, I found myself rebelling.

"O Lord," I prayed, "my mother as an ordained minister has given 60 years in work for Your kingdom. Can't there be something better for her?" I knew how she loved solitude, disliked the noise of a television set, and had always been independent as a professional woman. I longed for her to have a better situation for the closing time of her life. All she said to us was, "This is my Father's will for me. I accept it." But I was not so sure.

I spent a prayerful but very restless night after we left her. I had tried to care for her for a month but could not physically continue. I felt completely helpless.

The next morning I was up early. Because of the location of the nursing home, we were staying with a friend 60 miles from our home. She had a shelf of various coffee cups, so I decided to select one that morning. As I took it down and turned it around, I saw these words written on it: "I do my best and leave the rest to God." I was stunned for a moment as I realized this was a message from my Heavenly Father. I was also amused at the way in which He spoke to me—on a coffee cup. But I felt a sweet peace come over my unsettled spirit, and I had rest. This rest was almost like a cushion absorbing the tears and heartaches that were inevitable in dramatic changes such as this.

Yes, I agree—"Prayer is simply believing God to supply what is needed to fulfill His will."* That kind of faith opens the heart to rest.

The cycle of victorious living is constantly repeated. Life moves in cycles. It seems that we no sooner handle one problem or one situation than another one arises. Although our relationship with God is not disturbed, the enemy tries with each new situation to create fret. Repeatedly we turn from the possibility of fret to *commitment* of the new situation, *trusting* that He who has helped us thus far will continue to help, and *praising* Him for victory. Thus, we move back into a state of rest. The flight pattern of a bird seems always changing, yet it is a series of life patterns. He flies in and up and around and back again in the process of getting food or protecting his mate or seeking a place to stop and sing. It's the nature of birdlife to do this. Our life is never static. It's always moving and therefore always open to invasion, suggestion, and temptation. But our "flight pattern" can always end in rest—that's the glorious truth.

> *My heart is resting, O my God;*
> *I will give thanks and sing.*
> *My heart is at the Secret Source*
> *Of every precious thing.*
> —Anna L. Waring

When God gives us a directive, remember that unbelief, or even doubt, can cause fret and throw us out of the cycle. J. B. Phillips translates Heb. 4:11-12, "Let us then be eager to know this rest for ourselves, and let us beware that no one

*Robert E. Coleman, *Personal Prayer Journal* (Minneapolis: World Wide Publications, 1994), 42.

misses it through falling into . . . s[o]me kind of unbelief . . . For the Word that God speaks is alive and active; it cuts more keenly than any two-edged sword: it strikes through to the place where soul and spirit meet, to the innermost intimacies of a man's being: it examines the very thoughts and motives of a man's heart."

Unbelief keeps us from cashing in on our benefits. It is a blinding sin that robs us of what God has prepared for us. But living in *relaxed readiness*, "the *r*s of rest," brings a persistent spirit of faith.

The Ps. 37 rest is also a *creative rest*. It consists of enthusiastic *expectation*. Rhoda, written about in Acts 12, had this kind of feeling. While the Early Church was praying constantly for Peter, Rhoda's spirit of expectation enabled her to hear his knock at the gate. Probably the others were praying so loudly that they could not hear the answer. Do we sometimes pray ourselves out of faith? It is quite possible. The disciples doubted, but she kept insisting that it was so. She knew the rest of faith.

The story of the imprisonment of John the Baptist gives us another picture of how doubt can rob us of our rest. Out of his dark, cold cell, John sent a question to Jesus: "Are you the one who was to come, or should we expect someone else?" (Matt. 11:3). This was an honest question. John wanted to be sure. How patient Jesus is with our questions!

Rather than rebuke John, Jesus gave this beautiful answer: "Go and tell John what you hear and see—that blind men are recovering their sight, cripples are walking, lepers being healed, the deaf hearing, the dead being raised to life and the good news is being given to those in need. And happy is the man who never loses his faith in me" (Matt. 11:4-6, Phillips).

Rest not only means *readiness* and *expectation* but also implies a steady *satisfaction*. God's sanctifying grace establishes us in His rest and brings lifelong satisfaction in Him. As Paul was nearing the end of his earthly life, he expressed his satisfaction with these words: "However, I consider my life worth nothing to me, if only I may finish the race and complete the task the Lord Jesus has given me—the task of testifying to the gospel of God's grace" (Acts 20:24). God's rest brings great inner poise.

In 1953 we returned to India for our second term. As field superintendent, I was responsible for many important and far-reaching decisions. A month later I was scheduled to conduct the preachers' yearly meeting. It was a major project, and I sincerely wanted God's plan for that conference.

I set to work in prayer and preparation with true commitment. I had attended many preachers' meetings and had a fair idea of what I wanted. But it seemed that every plan or idea turned to sawdust in my hands. I prayed all the more, for time was running out. I thought I was seeking to be sure His plans were mine. Eventually I realized it was just the opposite: I wanted to know that my plans were His.

In the midst of my frustration I gave myself to fasting as well as prayer. I searched God's Word for a special, divine signal. Certainly the words of Paul in Ephesians or Philippians would spawn a great idea. But those usually rich letters seemed Sahara-like to me. After a while my feverishness subsided, and I quieted myself before the Lord. It was obvious that *I* was in the center, and God had to get me out of the way.

In a time of quiet meditation, God prompted me to read in Exodus. In chapter 33 I found my oasis. Moses was in a comparable situation. He was under the cloudy pillar in the Tabernacle, and all the people were standing in their tent doors, waiting for God's Word through him. Moses spoke with great boldness as he prayed, "Teach me your ways" (v. 13).

The startling answer God gave to Moses was my answer too. All the burden of personal responsibility came tumbling down as I read, "My Presence will go with you, and I will give you rest" (v. 14).

His presence would go with me to the preachers' meeting. What more did I need? As I read the full passage, I realized that *presence* and *rest* and *glory* were almost synonymous. My heart was swept with praise and thanksgiving as I placed everything completely into God's hands.

Out of that 1953 preachers' meeting came a glory of revival that I have never experienced before or since. God's rest leads us to *triumph:*

> **R**eadiness
> **E**xpectation
> **S**atisfaction
> **T**riumph

The Ps. 37 rest is also beautifully pictured in Ps. 23. The following is titled "23rd Psalm for Busy People":

> *The Lord is my Pacesetter; I shall not rush.*
> *He makes me stop and rest for quiet intervals.*
> *He provides me with images of stillness, which restore my serenity.*
> *He leads me in ways of efficiency, through calmness of mind,*
> *And His guidance is peace.*
> *Even though I have a great many things to accomplish each day*
> *I will not fret, for His presence is here.*
> *His timelessness, His all-importance, will keep me in balance.*
> *He prepares refreshment and renewal in the midst of my activity*
> *By anointing my mind with His oils of tranquility.*
> *My cup of joyous energy overflows.*
> *Surely harmony and effectiveness shall be the fruits of my hours,*
> *For I shall walk in the peace of my Lord, and dwell in His house forever.*
>
> —Toki Miyashina

7

Jesus Is Lord

In 1954 during a wonderful outpouring of the Holy Spirit in revival in India, my wife and I were asked to share our experiences with another denomination. We were invited to a well-known hospital compound in Vrindāvan, a city full of idols. From the very first meeting, the Holy Spirit came. People were gripped by a spirit of openness and honesty, and prayers of many years were answered.

One afternoon I sat in the old mission bungalow with a gentleman converted to Christianity from Hinduism. There was an air of brooding about this scholarly man as he rocked back and forth in a hand-carved rocker. The more we discussed things of the Spirit, the more I sensed his deep dissatisfaction. He had come with a need.

After a few minutes, he leaned forward and looked at me intently. "Mr. Lee," he said, "I want you to tell me what total freedom means. I don't want your answer today. I want you to think about it and to pray about it. God has told me that you can give me the answer I need."

I was quite astonished. I promised him I would certainly pray about it and mind the Spirit. I went to our room, feeling mystified and troubled. What could I teach this great scholar? Soon I was comforted to realize the answer would come from Christ, not from me.

Two days later we returned to the historic old parlor. With a look of anticipation, he sat down in the same old rocking chair.

I waited a bit before speaking. Finally I said, "The answer seems so simple I'm hesitant to give it; yet I feel it's from the Lord."

"I know it's from the Lord," he promptly replied. "Let's hear it. I'm ready."

"Well, it's simply this: If the Son makes you free, you are free indeed. That means *freedom IN your circumstances, not freedom FROM circumstances.*"

He closed his eyes, leaned back in his chair for a few seconds, and then said, "Say that again."

"God wants to free you where you are, not take you out of the situation," I replied.

"Say it once again."

I repeated the thought.

With tears filling his dark eyes, he reached over and placed my hand in his strong, brown hands. "I accept it. That's the truth I need: freedom *in* your circumstances, not freedom *from* circumstances. Thank you." With a look of peace, he said, "I'll do it. I'll accept what must be accepted and find my freedom right where I am." He walked from the room with determination.

Later I discovered how beautifully the Holy Spirit had guided. This man was embroiled in a delicate and difficult family situation from which there was no escape. God showed him that the relief he needed was within himself, in his attitude toward the situation. Through a marvelous series of events, God worked things out beyond our asking or thinking.

The entire week was full of miracles. When it came time to leave, Mr. C—— rode with me in a horse-drawn tonga to the station. We shared the rich experiences of the week. Our fellowship in Christ was very warm. As the train was approaching the station, he turned to me rather abruptly and said, "Do you know what *Jesus is Lord*' really means?"

Sensing he had a personal answer, I asked, "What *does* it mean?"

"Well, *Jesus is Lord*' means He is my Owner, He is my Possessor, and He is my Dispossessor!"

Later in the night I thought about what he had said to me. E. Stanley Jones often said, "Jesus is Lord" with three fingers held high. Mr. C—— was giving names to those three fingers: Owner, Possessor, Dispossessor. I recalled the words of Job: "The LORD gave and the LORD *has taken away;* may the name of the LORD be praised" (1:21, emphasis added).

Job's testimony came after he had lost everything dear to him. He suffered bereavement, questions, misunderstanding, and bodily pain. But he blessed the name of the Lord. Though God had dispossessed him of all he owned, God had not disinherited him. The thing that mattered most remained—his relationship with his God.

Jesus is Lord is the great center of the cycle of victorious living. The key phrase from each of these four verses in Ps. 37 is "in [or to] the Lord." Commit *to the Lord;* trust *in the Lord;* delight *in the Lord;* rest *in the Lord.* This kind of living demands a sacramental view of life; everything must be done *to* the Lord. All that we are and do must respond affirmatively to the question "Is Jesus Christ the Center?"

E. Stanley Jones says that either Jesus is Lord *of* all, or He is not Lord *at* all. We cannot truthfully say, "Jesus means everything to me," if anything else is at the center of our lives. No matter how good our center may be, *if it is other than Jesus Christ,* it is not good enough. Whatever is at the center will control us, just as the hub controls the wheel.

Jesus is Lord was the creed of the Early Church, and since the Resurrection it is the great recurring theme in the symphony of the kingdom of God. It is still true for today's generation. If Jesus is Lord, life has meaning. He makes the difference between victory and defeat, between hope and despair, between life and death.

Too many circles of philosophical thought end in a "horror of darkness." The inability to communicate is one of the great problems of existentialism. Like a figure in a nightmare, man wants to cry out, but he has no voice. Jesus Christ gives us a voice, a purpose, a center by *being* the Voice, the Purpose, the Center.

The rich young man came running to Jesus. "'Good teacher,' he asked, 'what must I do to inherit eternal life?'" (Mark 10:17). He was sincerely troubled; he really wanted an answer.

Jesus looked on him with love, longing for him to fulfill his personhood. But the young man lacked one thing—allegiance to Christ. He would have to cut off all his earthly supports. Christ placed His finger on the vulnerable spot as He said, "Go, sell . . . give . . . Then come, follow me" (v. 21). The young man turned away sorrowfully. His center was self, and self controlled him. The words of Christ were action words that demanded a reversal of direction, a cross he was not willing to take.

Everything we *commit* is to the Cross; our *trust* is wholly in the Cross; our *delight* is in the Cross. As Paul said in Gal. 6:14, "May I never boast except in the cross of our Lord Jesus Christ, through which the world has been crucified to me, and I to the world." And our *rest,* too, is in the finished work of Christ on the Cross, for "every day we experience something of the death of Jesus, so that we may also show the power of the life of Jesus in these bodies of ours" (2 Cor. 4:10, Phillips).

It is through Him that "we live and move and *have our being*" (Acts 17:28, emphasis added). He gets into the inner parts of our personalities and creates a growing edge that continues until life is over. We are ever discovering our potential in Him and moving in a "divine crescendo" more and more to the perfect day. He heals our wounds and is continually helping us with our weaknesses, our complexes, our maladjustive impulses, and our damaged emotions. Rom. 8:11 says, "Once the Spirit of him who raised Christ Jesus from the dead lives within you he will, by that same Spirit, bring to your whole being, yes even your mortal bodies, new strength and vitality" (Phillips). The Holy Spirit is the greatest creative force in the world.

When Jesus is Lord, He guides us in our interpersonal relationships. He controls our families, our friendships, our attitudes, and our activities. When the risen Lord met Peter on the shore, the disciple was quite disturbed about John. He said to Christ, "Lord, what about him?" (John 21:21). J. B. Phillips translates Christ's answer, "If it is my wish . . . for him to stay until I come, is that your business, Peter? You must follow me" (v. 22). That puts an end to many unsettling matters—"You must follow me." Any attitude, any liaison, any transaction that keeps us from following Christ is out of bounds to us. *Jesus is Lord* leads through a narrow path to life eternal. There is no room for extra baggage.

Who knows our weaknesses better than the Holy Spirit? He is constantly at work to perfect us. J. B. Phillips translates 2 Cor. 4:7, 5, "This priceless treasure we hold, so to speak, in common earthenware—to show that the splendid power of it belongs to God and not to us. . . . For it is Christ Jesus as Lord whom we preach, not ourselves."

In an age of humanism, the Spirit teaches us that He is Host of this universe. We are merely His guests, yet He allows us to carry around this great treasure in our earthly bodies so that we might always be reminded of our dependence on God.

What difference does it make? Listen to these words farther on: "We are hard-pressed on all sides, but we are never frustrated; we are puzzled, but never in despair. We are persecuted, but are never deserted: we may be knocked down but we are never knocked out!" (4:8-9, Phillips). He gives us the ability to keep on going in His power.

Several years ago my usual pastoral duties included visiting in the homes of my parishioners. I sat down to an evening meal with my family one night, preoccupied about the calling I planned to do. Suddenly our younger son said, "Dad, do you really have to go out again tonight?"

His question cut into my thinking like a knife. No, I really did not *have* to go calling that night. I decided that the most important thing for me that evening was to remain at home with my family. It was a great relief to stop, regain a relaxed spirit, and enjoy the ones I love. The Kingdom would go on, for *Jesus* is Lord, not I!

The cycle of victorious living requires a teachable spirit. In this way we cultivate "a heart at leisure from itself." We have an inner poise and security from which we fulfill Christ's command to *go,* to *tell,* and to *do.*

When Jesus is Lord, we know the deep meaning of the hymn:

> *In service which Thy love appoints*
> *There are no bonds for me;*
> *My secret heart is taught the truth*
> *That makes Thy children free;*
> *A life of self-renouncing love*
> *Is one of liberty.*
> —Anna L. Waring

The adventure of life in the cycle never ends. There will be new insights, new joys, and new discoveries. This total concept describes what life is like walking with Jesus Christ. It is life on tiptoes of excitement in the Spirit.

Have a great time in *your* adventure in Christ, in the cycle of victorious living. Someday we will talk it over together with our wonderful Lord, who is the Center of everything; for "he is before all things, and in him all things hold together. And he is the head of the body, the church; he is the beginning and the firstborn from among the dead, so that in everything he might have the supremacy. For God was pleased to have all his fullness dwell in him" (Col. 1:17-19).

Jesus is Lord!

8

It Works

Of all the experiences of parenting, patience to follow the directions is one of the most challenging. Most parents prefer to assemble their child's new toy from experience or simply by trying to figure it out. But if we painstakingly read the directions, soon perseverance and cooperation pay off. When the newly assembled airplane zooms into loops around the backyard, there is a feeling of exhilaration for both parent and child—"We really made it work!"

All of us want a way of life that *works*. The cycle of victorious living works. It is a set of instructions based on the truth of God's Word. It opens the way to a new level of sanctified living.

My preaching on the cycle of victorious living has earned me the right to share in the lives of many people. Through much of my pastoral ministry, I preached this series once a year. The result has been repeated in many individual lives.

One elderly woman came to worship faithfully on Sunday mornings but, because of ill health, was unable to attend other services. She had been widowed for a number of years. While her husband was alive, he had almost wrapped her in tissue paper as he tenderly cared for her every need. After his death she lived much more marginally.

Not long after I had preached my sermon on the cycle of victorious living, I stepped up to her porch for a visit. I could hardly believe my ears. She was playing the piano and singing a hymn with great gusto.

I waited until she had finished a verse and then knocked. I was anxious to see the source of joy in this usually silent home. She came to the door with the glow of the music still on her face.

I said in amazement, "I didn't know you could sing and play so well. I really enjoyed that!"

"Come in, Pastor, and I'll tell you what's happened to me," she replied as she swung open the door. "After you preached your sermon on 'the cycle,' I knew there was something in that sermon for me. Since my husband died, I have gone on living, but more as an existence. New truth has come through to me, and now I'm really *alive!*" She whirled around on the piano stool, and we sang a duet of joy together.

Her health did not improve appreciably. In fact, in a subsequent examination her doctor told her he could not see what was keeping her alive. But she confided in me that everything was committed to the Lord, she was delighting in "the cycle," and that was reason enough to live. Years later she wrote to me: "The messages you gave, Brother Lee, on the 37th psalm still linger with me. Today is only the second time I have been out to church since Christmas, but through all the pain and suffering the blessed words linger with me, "Heaven will be worth it all."

Once the truth of this cycle becomes a way of life, it goes on and on through the years, regardless of circumstances.

Mrs. Lee and I had been asked to speak at a valentine banquet in a neighboring church. Afterward, a young woman I did not know said to me, "Let me tell you, Brother Lee—that cycle of victorious living really works!"

I was startled to hear this enthusiastic testimony from a stranger. "Now where did you hear that?" I asked, quite puzzled.

She opened her Bible where she had especially marked Ps. 37 and reminded me of an indoor camp meeting held in Norwalk, Calif., where I had been the speaker.

"You pulled out a large blackboard and drew the cycle on it and then proceeded to tell us how to live victoriously. I made up my mind that I had better get started in the cycle. That was six months ago, and my life has been completely changed ever since!"

The best part of that banquet for me was to see the woman's radiant face and to share in her joy as she reached a new level of Spirit-filled living.

A friend and I had spent many hours together as we prayed and believed for his spiritual release. The cycle had been a prominent part of our times of sharing. Through God's Word and especially through Ps. 37, he had found many answers for his badly shattered life.

In trying to find his way, he had wisely sought professional help. One day during our regular visit he surprised me with an account of his most recent session with his doctor. "Believe it or not, Pastor, I took along this little diagram of the cycle and showed it to my doctor."

I was surprised. Most patients would not have this much courage! "What did he think?" I asked.

"The doctor looked at the cycle as I explained it to him and what it had done for me, and he said, 'This truth is psychologically sound and seems to be a great answer.'

"Then I smiled as I quietly told him the whole principle was found in the Bible, in the 37th psalm!"

I walked into a hospital room where a teenager was lying flat on her back with a broken leg hoisted up in a splint. An arm was also broken, and her head was severely lacerated. The car in which she had been riding had been hit by a train, and the young driver had been killed. I prayed a prayer of thanksgiving that this girl was alive. She was a new convert and was radiant in her newfound faith.

Several days later when I returned to see her, my attention was drawn to something hung above her door. There, staring her right in the face, was the diagram of the cycle of victorious living, which one of her friends had drawn for her.

"Linda," the friend had said to her, "this is what you need more than anything else right now!"

With youthful candor she admitted it was true as she added, "Pastor, it has lifted my spirits totally and taken my mind off myself. It is the best prescription of all!"

Several years following the Vietnam War, a young veteran in my church asked for an appointment with me. He sat across my desk from me, completely weighed down with burdens of home, family, and adjustments that only war veterans would understand. I let him fully unload and then asked him if he was familiar with the cycle of victorious living. I took out a small card on which the diagram was printed and shared it with him. Then I said, "Have you been filled with the Holy Spirit?"

He was silent for a few seconds. Although he had been brought up in the church and had learned a commanded discipline in the army, spiritually he was extremely undisciplined.

"No, Pastor, I don't believe I've ever asked the Holy Spirit to take over the center of my life," he said quite candidly. *"I've been the center."*

I showed him what it meant for Jesus Christ to be Lord of his life. Self had to be crucified in order for Christ to be Lord. A deliberate transaction was necessary.

Light came to him. He accepted it and surrendered to the Holy Spirit, confessing his need in prayer. Of course, the Holy Spirit came, and the man left my office delighting in the Lord. A few days later I met him again after the close of a service. He gripped my hand warmly as he said, "Pastor, it works!"

A member of my church narrowly escaped injury and death in an automobile accident. His brand-new car had been demolished. It was a miracle the man was alive.

"Were you wearing your seat belt?" I asked.

"I sure was!" he answered. "But let me tell you how that cycle of victorious living you preached about helped me in that nearly fatal accident. After the impact, I skidded across the intersection. As I came to a stop, I realized I was apparently not seriously injured, but my shiny new car was a wreck. In those first stunned seconds I found myself committing the entire situation to the Lord with a calmness that could come only from the Divine.

"In fact, I was so calm that I was able to help the other man involved make out his report. He was greatly upset and nervous.

"The next day I called at his home to see how he was doing and helped him with more paperwork. He looked at me in amazement as he asked, 'Why are you doing this for me? You have every reason to be doing just the opposite!'

"Then in a flash came the opportunity to explain to this man what Jesus Christ and His peace meant to me. And, Pastor," he added, "the cycle was there in my mind the moment I needed it, and I never had a fretful minute during that entire experience!"

Perhaps this is what Will Huff meant when he talked about "nick-of-time grace" (from Heb. 4:16). It works!

A great example of living victoriously is found in Habakkuk. The prophet looked about and saw the oppression of his people; he looked up and saw the inscrutability of his God; he looked within and saw a living faith. Like David, his faith was his hope in this evil world.

The last three verses of this little book contain some of the most magnificent imaginative poetry in literature. They also constitute one of the strongest declarations of faith ever written—a moving testimony of the cycle of victorious living:

> Though the fig tree does not bud
> and there are no grapes on the vines,
> though the olive crop fails
> and the fields produce no food,
> though there are no sheep in the pen
> and no cattle in the stalls,
>
> yet I will rejoice in the LORD,
> I will be joyful in God my Savior.
> The Sovereign LORD is my strength;
> he makes my feet like the feet of a deer,
> he enables me to go on the heights *(Hab. 3:17-19)*.

The Lord God not only gives strength but also *is* strength. As we *commit, trust, delight,* and *rest* in the Lord, we are enabled to leap into the heights of God's grace and love, sharing in the heavenly places with our Lord Jesus Christ, "far above all rule and authority, power and dominion, and every title that can be given, not only in the present age but also in the one to come" (Eph. 1:21).

9

Timeless Psalm 37

Since the original publication of *The Cycle of Victorious Living* in 1971, there have been many opportunities for ever-relevant Ps. 37 to work in our lives. We have written about these experiences in our 1993 book *Committed to Grace*. But it seems appropriate to add some of these thoughts to this edition.

The message of *The Cycle of Victorious Living* is timeless. These words written by a friend in 1971 have been repeated in the lives of many others:

> By the time I had finished reading *The Cycle,* I could hardly contain myself. You have expressed that which I have believed and experienced ever since my days at a Nazarene college. However, I have never read such truth, nor have I been able to express it as beautifully as you have. You have stripped the "victorious life" of all its meaningless and hard-to-define terms and clichés. It is an understandable and workable way of life that you have described. I believe that it is through insights like yours that Christ and the Bible continue to be relevant in our rapid and ever-changing society. I am convinced that it is concepts like those you expressed in your book that provide the permanence against all "future shock."

Even so—speak to us, Holy Spirit.

It has been God's grace that has enabled us to live out Ps. 37 when *fret* would take over. These phrases have become guideposts for our Spirit-filled lives:

"If you can't change it, commit it."

"Jesus is Lord, Owner, Possessor, Dispossessor."

"Fret is spiritual heartburn."

"Nothing pleases God like our praise."

"Rest from friction, not from action."

"Trusting when we don't understand delights our Heavenly Father."

We recently celebrated our 55th wedding anniversary. At the family gathering our grandson asked us the secret of being happily married for such a long time. Mutual love and respect, plus prayer together for God's guidance in many decisions, are foundation stones for a solid marriage. We reminisced fondly about our early days—both good and bad.

In our first year of marriage, we learned the secret of "trust and obey." We prayed in our food. Our first pastorate gave us a pulpit but not much else. Like birds of prey, we watched for the mailman, hoping someone felt led to send us a check! Ministers' wives did not earn money in secular positions in those days. On our knees we learned God provides, but we also learned there is a lot of *doing without*. It's a lesson we've never forgotten. The less you have, the less you need to protect.

After returning in 1959 from our years as missionaries in India, we learned again the secret of not fretting and trusting only in the Lord. We brought with us three children and a rocking chair, but little else. We had no home and no car. There were days when doubts like the birds of prey over Abraham's sacrifice swooped over us. We had to refuse to fret and to lean hard on our Lord. In God's time, all was provided.

One day a bright light shone into our waiting hearts as the Spirit whispered, "You have My will *for today*." God's plans unfolded in a surprising manner. We pastored Nampa, Idaho, First Church of the Nazarene for six fine years and then served a long pastorate at First Church of the Nazarene in Pasadena, Calif.

Several years ago I got a call from a lady who ordered a number of the *Cycle* books as a study guide for a group she taught at Robert Schuller's Crystal Cathedral. "You might like to know," she said, "I teach a class for patients with cancer, and we find our answer to our needs in your book."

I have a doctor friend who keeps a large supply of my book in his office to give to patients whose needs are other than physical.

The Cycle of Victorious Living has been translated into several languages, the latest being Hindi, a language in India spoken by millions. Ps. 37 will burn its truth into many seeking hearts there.

A few years after receiving his graduate degree from Fuller Theological Seminary, a friend of mine started a church in a mountain community. While in Pasadena First Church he became intrigued with the cycle of victorious living. He earned his living in Bishop, Calif., as a counselor, using his degree in psychology. He introduced the Native Americans in his church to the *Cycle* book, and they were enthusiastic. He called for 50 books and had a special seminar with them. In the Native American culture, most of their thinking revolves in a circular form. They found the cycle of victorious living linking into their very thinking and reaction processes. Amazing!

The 444 days our son Gary was a hostage in Iran were truly days of commitment. "If you can't change it, commit it." How often I've said that when preaching on the cycle. When Hazel got a call one day from a local reporter wanting an interview, she knew I was reluctant. Then the reporter said, "I've read his book and wonder if it works now!" Yes, I gave the interview. Yes, it still worked!

I also placed an American flag in front of my home each morning as a symbol of my trust. We learned during that long year to simply "do the next thing." God provided the grace.

When the hostages returned January 20, 1981, we were grateful we had trusted when we could not understand. We will never understand all that God allows us to go through. But He promises that we will not go through it alone.

Six years ago Gary had surgery for colon cancer. As a result of that surgery, his travel days for the United States State Department ceased. Today he is faced with many changes in his lifestyle. Our hearts at times cry out *"Why?"* After the ordeal he endured in Iran, why this? The heavens are silent. There is no answer. We learn to accept what we can't understand. How often we've quoted the title of a recent book by Robert Schuller, *Life Is Not Fair, but God Is Good.*

Facing retirement took a special grace and trust. Having had such a challenging, thriving pastorate in Pasadena made the unknown future seem more bleak. But knowing it was God's will and the proper timing, we obeyed.

But talk about surprises! Because of the extensive "Cassettes for Christ" ministry, we've been going into open doors all over the world these past 10 years. *Trust* and *obey* are little words in print but contain the true secret of victorious living. We must keep close enough to the Spirit to hear His whisper: "This is the way; walk in it" (Isa. 30:21). We never know what's around the corner, but we know who is there.

And so we will continue to commit, trust, delight, and rest until "the world is wound up." We are told by Jesus in John 14:1-3, "Do not let your hearts be troubled. *Trust* in God; *trust* also in me. In my Father's house are many rooms; if it were not so, I would have told you. I am going there to prepare a place for you. And if I go and prepare a place for you, I will come back and take you to be with me that you also may be where I am" (emphasis added).

Someday our table in God's kingdom will be ready, our room prepared, and in His time He will come for us.